Dr. Mary Speed, is a person whom I have grown to love and cherish; she is my Guardian Angel. When I feel like my world is a bunch of mixed nuts, from out of nowhere she gives me encouragement to keep on keeping on. In this lifetime, I am so blessed to have met and come to know her.

Through *Mixed Nuts* you will too.—Rosalind D. Hayes, LPN, Louisiana

Therapy is much like weightlifting for your soul. The muscles of your mood gain memory and strength with each session. No one specific regimen works for everyone, but when you find your partner in counseling, you will begin a great work. Please consider that everyone needs a periodic workout. Therapy need not be a response to an acute event or trauma. Life is a series of changes and transitions that make demands on one's inner strength. Dr. Mary Speed shares her experiences, and I would be surprised if the reader of *Mixed Nuts* does not get a little exercise in the process.

-Eric N. Tabor, MD, Northshore Dermatology

Dr. Mary Speed is an amazing woman, whom I am honored to have in my life. From the moment I met her, I was captivated by her knowledge and experience. In her book, *Mixed Nuts*; Mary shares her skills with a combination of experience, understanding of life and unconditional positive regard for others. We are blessed to have a glimpse of Dr. Speed's wisdom in her book.—Dana Baker, Assistant Supervisor, Rural Unit, Saskatoon Ministry of Social Services, Saskatchewan

Mixed Nuts

Dr. Mary Speed

abbott press®
A DIVISION OF WRITER'S DIGEST

Mixed Nuts

Author Photograph - Katie Speed Richard
Photographs - Erin Reilly Bailey @ www.eriphotography.com
Book Cover - Elizabeth Kepper Brown @ www.EKBrownArt.com

Abbott Press books may be ordered through booksellers or by contacting:

Abbott Press
1663 Liberty Drive
Bloomington, IN 47403
www.abbottpress.com
Phone: 1-866-697-5310

ISBN: 978-1-4582-0134-8 (sc)
ISBN: 978-1-4582-0135-5 (hc)
ISBN: 978-1-4582-0133-1 (e)

Library of Congress Control Number: 2011961744

Printed in the United States of America

Abbott Press rev. date: 01/05/2012

For Anonymous

CONTENTS

LIST OF PHOTOGRAPHS

PREFACE

I have been a practicing clinician for sixteen years. And, in the years before schooling and licensure, people told me their stories. I am privileged to hear.

I'm not sure how all that happens, the duet of one talking and one listening. The natural ebb and not-so-natural flow of spiritual connectedness that transpire in therapy is something more than two people talking.

As in music, the instance of someone beginning a vocal solo and someone accompanying knowing exactly the moment to begin the accompaniment is a mystery and precise. So is the connectedness that transpires in therapy.

My years of being the active listener for clients and colleagues, sometimes challenging voice to both, have brought stories to me. I respect and value the sacredness of their trust.

On occasion I have people ask me about medical issues, everything from pink eye to surgery, and I say, "I'm not that kind of doctor."

I don't do surgery to remove parts or scar tissue, yet that is what my practice is about. I work with clients to discover and explore injurious parts and work toward healing.

The stories and commentaries that follow are real. For respect of confidence, no person except my family will be recognizable. Excerpts are related to clients who are the inspiration behind the column that I write for in *Sophisticated Woman*. All clients are unique, yet all have the same desire: they want something, more often *someone*, to change. If you have ever been interested in therapy, this book is for you.

My family has nut trees: walnut, pecan, chestnut, and hickory. I've learned that nothing of sustenance can happen without opening up. The wealth is inside.

FORWARD

In this very revealing work, Dr. Mary Speed is able to accomplish the unique task of providing concise, yet in-depth descriptions of many of the most difficult clinical situations that a "real world" therapist is faced with on a daily basis. Through very poignant case vignettes, Dr. Speed introduces the reader to struggles that she has helped her patients with during her many years of practice. The reader is given the rare opportunity to experience what goes on during an actual therapy session. It is my hope as a clinician that the cases discussed herein will remove much of the mystery from therapy for those who read this work. Many individuals who would benefit from therapy are hesitant to enter treatment because they are only aware of the "Hollywood" versions of therapy that they have seen on television or in movies. They perceive a therapist as the person sitting in a chair all the while scribbling on a pad and asking them "how do you feel about that?" to everything they say, which could not be farther from the reality of what happens between therapist and patient during a true therapy session. This book demonstrates both the essential collaborative energy between therapist and patient, as well as exploring the levels of trust that must be present for therapy to be truly effective. This book also portrays the humorous moments in therapy that are always so healing for individuals yet somehow are not always given their due. There are so many points in this book where the reader cannot help but smile and acknowledge that "yeah, I've been there too."

In **Mixed Nuts**, Dr. Speed demonstrates both her considerable skill as a therapist and her compassion as a human being, traits which are essential in a psychotherapist. Dr. Speed has worked extensively with individuals from a variety of situations. She has worked with children and adults who have suffered through horrible traumas and helped them recover their lives. In addition to being an outstanding clinician, Dr. Speed has served as an educator and shared her experiences and clinical knowledge with the next generation of therapists. Her work with the underprivileged and the chronically mentally ill has certainly been a source of inspiration to me on both the personal and professional level. I congratulate her on completing this most compelling book and anxiously await her next publication.

I heartily and enthusiastically recommend this book to everyone's reading list.

R. Timothy Brown, MD
Child, Adolescent and Adult Psychiatrist

INTRODUCTION

Change is uncomfortable. When I was a child and had some invisible ache, my mom would say, "This is not a worry; this is a growing pain."

I think she was exactly right. We can't grow into our adult selves without discomfort; growing up requires stretching of internal and external extremities.

No one—person, place, business, or thing—is exempt. Like time, change moves on a continuum; unlike time, some changes can be brutally abrupt.

Life transitions are not a recognized diagnosis yet give cause for symptoms of despair and anxiety.

My therapeutic goal is worthy, ambitious . . . unrealistic. I want to alleviate suffering. The problem with this stance is that fixing is outside the scope of my responsibility and capacity.

Proverbs 23:7a reads, "As a man thinketh in his heart, so is he." Cognitive distortions may cause a successful man to feel inadequate and shamed. Therapy may allow him to open doors within himself to accept his success without psychological flagellation.

ADDICTION

A beautiful young woman came to see me for therapy. I noticed her confident handshake, the sparkling multi-carat gemstone ring. I wondered, *What can it be that brings this extraordinary person to therapy?* She didn't know exactly, but she had an *ic*. Her chief concern was that she thought she might be doing too much of something; a vague description, at first.

She had *an addition* that had gotten out of control. What addictions have in common are that they numb and keep the addict distanced from ics. She had the icky sense that something was off.

People craving suffer great shame over their incapacity to stop themselves. They spin around like a hamster on a wheel: indulge—feel ashamed (ic)-indulge-numb-shame (ic)-indulge-numb. Desperate to get rid of the ic, they continue indulging and are legion in **numb**er, both in consumption and people so affected.

My client described a memory of herself at five years of age, sitting in front of a television and crying. Her friend had moved away, and she didn't have words for her feelings. Her mom came into the room, saw her crying, and thrust fresh-baked cookies and milk at her. She quit crying.

She numbed and disengaged herself from others and self and grew unavailable to engage emotional support. She had a compulsion to curb her feelings. Eventually, she was unresponsive to her own needs, unaware of time lapsed; she missed cues that she was sleepy or ill.

Addiction came easy. When disappointed, she substituted something and avoided facing hurt.

My client learned early to eat her way out of tragedy. Her mother's response to grief was: "Your friend moved away? Don't cry. I'm busy now. Here, eat these cookies." Message: Hide your feelings. Your feelings are making me uncomfortable. I don't have time for you.

This courageous, young woman did the work to address her addictions. She admitted that she had come to therapy because of something that had caught her eye. She had seen a child reaching toward a cookie jar, and it was as if time stopped. She focused, spellbound, frame by frame on the scene, and she saw herself as a child doing the same thing. She was angry and did some mom-bashing, saying, "My mother ought to have hugged me and held me, not stuffed me." She worked through blaming her mother and herself, hating cookies and loving cookies. She worked through hating the times she reached out for one thing, realizing she had wanted something else. She cried . . . a lot.

Early in my practice, I became extremely uncomfortable when clients cried. I used to try to cheer them up so they would stop crying. I've learned. Clients taught me to be silent and let their tears flow. Sometimes, after the sobbing subsides, I ask a client, "If your tears could talk, what would they say?"

The young woman's tentative admission that she had an addiction led to self-discovery. Until therapy, she had hidden her upsetting feelings and squelched her awareness of the "Stuff it, and leave me alone" messages. Though her weight was never the focus of our sessions, during the year of therapy, she lost seventy-five pounds. Two weeks into therapy, she announced that she was getting her hair cut and going to the gym. She became less angry, grew in awareness of herself. Losing weight caused her to "expose" herself and be vulnerable, available.

ANOREXIA NERVOSA, BULIMIA NERVOSA

Group therapy for anorexia nervosa or bulimia nervosa is potentially counterproductive. These highly intelligent clients are inclined to make weight loss a competition.

I believe foods that ensure physical well-being also enhance psychological wellness. A void of self-worth, however, may lead to self-induced malnourishment.

Eating disorders are troubling. The client is physically sound, yet unbalanced in her self-perception and stoically capable of starving herself to death.

One of a child's first steps of independence is food choice. Eating maturation may be associated with power plays and power struggles. Controlling food intake and output can be pathologically empowering.

Anorexia nervosa and bulimia nervosa are life-threatening disorders. Karen Carpenter, Princess Diana, and many more have suffered, and others continue to be afflicted. The way to recovery is fraught with setbacks. The likelihood is that, when feeling powerless or violated, these individuals will resort to this pattern of unhealthy coping. These disorders appear addictive; consequently, one of the treatments is to interrupt the cycle. After meals, engaging in conversation with the bulimic individual prohibits his or her immediate purging. For someone with anorexia, having an available abundance of non-threatening foods, which are acceptable to her such as nonfat yogurts and cut vegetables may encourage eating. Telling someone who has anorexia that the few extra pounds look good on her is counterproductive and may cause a relapse. It is better to say, "I enjoy spending time with you."

When someone with anorexia nervosa appears pleased and says that she has gained weight, beware-she probably has a weigh-in and has consumed gallons of water.

The eldest of Pat Boone's four daughters, Cherry, had anorexia nervosa. In *Starving for Attention*, she relates that after years of failed treatments, one professional finally said something that made a difference. What he said freed her of the inadequacies she felt over her failure to be recover perfectly. Her doctor, Dr. Raymond E. Vath, said, "If an activity is worth doing, it is worth doing poorly."

For Cherry, this meant that if she fouled up, ate too much, or purged, she didn't have to give up. She was worth making the effort. She was free to try again. Her less than best counted. She didn't have to do everything perfectly; she was relieved from the pressure and tyranny of perfectionism.

Individuals with these disorders often are the perfect sons and daughters. They make excellent grades, bring home ribbons and trophies, and are highly intelligent.

People with anorexia nervosa and bulimia nervosa need to hear repeatedly that they are worthy and that their acceptance is not performance-based. Their imperfections are acceptable. Their value is not measured in accomplishments or pounds; separate from what she does; accepted for who she is. Worthy.

~3~

ANXIETY

Freud said that the tension between what a person is inclined to do and what society will accept creates anxiety. Freud would be surprised I think to see that societal acceptance of behavior has not curtailed anxiety.

One may have a realistic foreboding that something is about to go wrong, and any efforts to avert the sense of impending disaster may cause apprehension. Anxiety may be optimal and helpful, inspiring one to prepare (study for a test, practice a speech) or anxiety may be unhelpful, which may cause one to freeze and fail to perform.

A client fearing performance failure came to therapy because of anxiety over giving a speech. She gives excellent talks and trainings, she explained, but was suffering over the notion of giving a speech in a public forum because she did not entirely know her audience.

Successful people have more anxiety. People who do things in the world have reasonable worry. She, however, was agonizing.

She was faced with a compelling worry, so we developed a plan to empower her to diminish her distress. I admitted that she could not know for certain that others would make things right for her. She could only make certain that things were right within herself, which allowed her a reasonable a reasonable expectation that her efforts would produce a good outcome.

I asked her to notice the nuances within herself that bid her caution. She visualized aloud giving her speech and worked on her tone, until she felt a nudge to stop. Sometimes the cues are subtle; they may seem out of reach and not easy to verbalize. She knew something was nudging at her. I asked her to pause and ask herself, "What do I expect my eyes to see? What do I expect my ears to hear?"

She confessed. "I see people looking away from me and talking to each. I hear people laughing."

I asked, "And how do you feel seeing and hearing these images?"

She said, "Dirty."

Before addressing that bomb, I said, "Have you ever turned away from a speaker and talked to someone sitting near you?"

Client: "Oh, yes!"

Me: "And?"

Client: "Usually," she explained, "I'm saying something like, 'Did you hear that? That's an excellent idea!'"

Me: "Has this happened with trainings you've given? People talk to each other in the audience?"

Client: "Yes, often. They might miss a point and ask their friends to repeat it."

Me: "And this," I probed, "makes you feel dirty?"

Client: "No."

I was quiet.

Five minutes passed before either of us spoke.

She said, "I remember now, when I was in high school, I had to give a speech on economics. I had actually memorized the speech, but before I reached for page nine of my speech, I introduced the next topic—and page nine wasn't there. I didn't know what to say, and . . . I started my period. I was mortified."

"Have you talked about this before?" I asked.

Client: "No."

Me: "How do you feel now on the scale of dirty? One being the most vile to ten being as clean as the driven snow?"

Bewildered, she said, "Damn, I don't feel dirty at all."

"And this is because," I explained, "the power of that secret is no more. What do you want to say to your high school self that you needed to hear that day but no one said?"

I directed her to speak to an empty chair or to me. She looked at the empty chair.

"Honey," she said, "you worked so hard on that speech. I am so proud of you. Probably half the girls in the room were on their periods too. That's how it is with girls. You didn't do anything to be ashamed of . . ."

Attending to the information coming from within allowed to make informed choices and lessened her anxiety. We went to the center where she was to speak, and we checked the sound and lights. I listened to her practice her speech, and I purposefully ignored her. I looked at the ceiling, hummed, and rolled my eyes. She kept giving her speech. She worked to create self-confidence, and this magnified her assurance.

Cultivating a sense of awareness can help you give a speech, and it can also save your life. Criminals count on people being distracted. That's why it's not a great idea to walk into alleys, blindly texting as you go.

~4~

ASHES TO ASHES

A clinician came in, I thought at first to visit. I was flattered, and I eyed her with wonder. She'd been a clinician for more than twenty years. I had heard about her work and was glad that she would drop in to see me, someone newer in the field. I was glad, that is, until she told me that she wanted to see me for therapy. She said—too easily, I thought—"I have cancer and am dying; I want you to help me get through it."

I thought, No. One, I don't like death; two, you look healthy; and three, you'll be judging my technique the whole time.

I said, "Okay." I then questioned myself. I hope she doesn't think I mean okay, like okie-dokie, you're dying, or *okay*, then, that's fine with me, or yes, my child, I give you permission to die. I said okay because I didn't have the words to say otherwise that would save me from the responsibility she was bringing to me.

We got through the emotional, psychological, and spiritual fumbling. She passed on, in peace (I hope), and left me angry that she had to die after all. Her visit wasn't some academic test. She was a real person with real needs who trusted me.

She couldn't control death. Nor can anyone pick the time or the circumstances of death. Responsible people try to make sure that others are not inconvenienced.

The clinician learned that she had few months to live. We prepared as though she were going on a journey. Times were set, but not certain as to when to discontinue home delivery of the newspaper. She did pick her clothes for her final public appearance at burial.

Others didn't know that the last time they saw her would be their last chance to visit with her. She acknowledged this definite, infinite end, and as she went about the last few months, she lived finally and fully.

Unlike other important events, she could not adequately prepare for the end. When she passed, she left things undone, and though she wished otherwise, others were be troubled and grieved.

She brought nothing into this world. We talked about that. She told me that others who had passed had left her things. Her first dog left her a love for brown-eyed creatures. Her grandpa left her knowing how to bait a fishhook.

She left me courage. She never gave up on living. Her body gave out on her.

Her estimation of me gave me confidence and humility. I learned to simply, profoundly value the moments spent in session.

~5~

COMPULSION

Everyone has a tendency to check on things. This is a non-issue unless these activities become compulsions that interfere with the activities of daily living. One might not get past washing hands to getting dressed and arriving at work on time. A few compulsions clients have presented are these:

One client presented with bleeding hands. At his worse, he vigorously washed his hands thirty-seven times a day. Refusing to touch doorknobs, he stood in front of doors waiting for someone to let him in or out, which made him late for events and once left him in a downpour of rain.

Another client kept going home to check on the iron she thought she might have left on. I told her to bring the iron with her.

One client couldn't stop praying, which seems a great gift. Yet, her praying kept her from engaging with others or dealing with issues. When her child or spouse wanted to talk to her, she would dismiss them, saying, "I have to pray now."

Compulsions are driven by obsessive thoughts. Ever lie in bed and suddenly think, Did I lock the door? You get up and check, see that the door is locked, and immediately feel less anxious. The lessening of anxiety is so compelling, some people will repeat the act, develop a pattern of behavior, and engage in rituals. People with compulsive behavior do the same thing many times over, so much so that they may stay awake all night, checking the door or counting steps.

Every successful person has some obsessive-compulsive tendencies, or as one of my former professors said, "Godly perseverance." Obviously, the A student does more fact-checking than does the C student. Good doctors check on their patients, all of them; they don't spend all their time checking on only one person.

My hand washing client was a checker and a counter 10 seconds washing per hand. Soap, check, each hand, check.

Combining his obsession with a greater anxiety made him better. His daughter had an eating disorder. With my guidance, they made a contract. If he washed his hands more than ten times a day, he agreed that she was allowed to skip all meals for the day. If she refused a meal, she agreed that he was allowed to wash his hands as many times as he wanted to that day. From the moment, they signed their contract, they both got better.

I counted on their evident love to save them. Had they not been kindly affectionate one toward the other, I would have taken a more traditional approach, which would have required therapy sessions more often and perhaps hospitalization for both.

~6~

COUPLES THERAPY

A client came for individual counseling and then changed her mind and wanted marital counseling. I gave her options. She could continue to see me for individual counseling, and if her husband would also participate, I would see them both for couples therapy. If her spouse would not agree to attend couples counseling, then she could continue to see me for individual counseling and go to another therapist for marital counseling.

When a person attends marital counseling without his or her spouse, more often than not, the couple will divorce. The person participating in therapy may feel more vested in the relationship. My hope was that this client would tell her spouse what I said, and he would grasp the seriousness of her decision.

Fortunately, her husband agreed to attend and participate in marital therapy. According to his wife, he was typically unwilling to try new things and this frustrated her. The world is dynamic, and she was afraid, I believe, that he was forcing her to move on without him. By agreeing to attend therapy with her, he gave her a clear indication of how much he valued their relationship.

16

I explored how to have them both be satisfied with the outcome of their therapy sessions. Did she need him to be more flexible? Did he need her to be more predictable?

Their communication styles were fostering conversation missteps, mishaps, confusion, conflict, hurt feelings, and now, the potential of the parting of ways. When she talked, she was like cement: her choices were still fluid with the possibility of being shaped into different formations. When he talked, in contrast, it was concrete: everything dry and set.

I considered how to resolve their growing differences. To move him into exploring other life choices, I could either introduce an idea that he might gradually accept or I could flood him with one option after the other.

I asked the couple if their children might participate in a session. They said yes. I then asked the parents if they would go on whatever weekly dates the children planned for them, and they agreed. I explained my plan to the children. "You are younger than your parents and know about how to have fun. Plan a fun date for your parents." Within the limits of budget, the children planned a date, and apparently for the first time, supported their parents' relationship. Maybe they understood what they all stood to lose. The children sent their parents out as individuals, but their parents came home a couple.

After the second date, the husband took charge of dating.

Couples have overt and covert rules of behavior. Some women believe that their men are supposed to "save" them. When things go wrong, these wives want their husbands to fix the problem. When men can't correct the problem, they typically want to flee their self-inflicted perception of powerlessness.

DEPRESSION

A pastor referred a client who came in presenting as lethargic, ambivalent.

Client: (stated without conviction): "I want to die."

Me: "You've never been dead, so I don't think you want to be dead. Seems rather that you don't want to live like this. Is that true?"

Client (said with a little more energy): "Yes."

Me: "Then you are in an excellent place to make a change. When is the last time you can recall feeling happy?" I listened closely to his response.

Client: "It was at my niece's graduation in May."

Me: "A time before that?"

Client: "Mother's Day."

Me: "What other happy times do you recall in May?"

I asked about other anniversary events. Fire in family home? Divorce? Dates of Births? Death of a parent? Type of death? Children of a parent who committed suicide might try on the anniversary of their parent's death.

This client refused to make any effort toward getting better. He minimized most suggestions that I offered in counseling and was noncompliant with completing homework assignments, including the smile task, which is something that is typically helpful to people struggling through depression. In someone sad, the act of smiling creates neurological dissonance, so that a person's mood usually alters in harmony with the smile.

This client would not smile. He came to therapy repeating every week his complaints of how everyone mistreated him all the time and had done so since his earliest remembrances. I asked if he could recall anyone at anytime showing him respect; he was speechless. I didn't interrupt his silence. Finally he said, "Well, I guess, you do."

I then said, "It's Christmas." I put my head down, shook it a bit, and looked up. "I dunno. Would you consider . . ." I put my head down again.

Client: (said with energy): "What?"

Me: "You've been weighted down so long, carrying what has to be a tremendous burden." I paused five-seconds. "You think you could give yourself one week of vacation?"

Client: "What?"

Me: "I mean every time an unpleasant thought comes to mind or anything at all that saddens you, put it aside for one week. Listen to only happy music. Entertain only positive conversations. I'd just like to see you have a bit of a break for the holidays. Think you could do it, for one week? Starting right now?"

He studied my face and then stood up, shook my hand, smiled, and said, "I'll do it."

In a week, he came back.

"How'd it go?" I asked.

He said, "I really liked it! Think it'd be okay if I do it next week too?"

His energy was up, and we walked for the remainder of his session. He gained mastery of managing his moods.

On occasion, I walk with clients. Those who are depressed usually talk more at the end of the walk than the beginning and clients who are manic talk more at the beginning of the walk than at the end. Walking modifies mood; I use these teachable moments and talk about how exercise improves mood. Exercise is the fourth tier in the foundation of mental health.

~8~

ELDERLY

A client saw me to talk about caring for her grandfather.

Usually the eldest daughter of the family becomes the caretaker of her aged mother and others.

This client was CO-caring in this capacity. She was helping her mother and taking on some responsibility for her maternal grandfather.

He was in good health but had failing hearing and sight. This is normal; most people need glasses before they need hearing aides. We addressed the days ahead. She was worried, and rightly so. Elderly Caucasian men are more likely than any other group to commit suicide. Older Americans are disproportionately likely to die by suicide.

- Of every 100,000 people ages 65 and older, 14.3 died by suicide in 2007. This figure is higher than the national average of 11.3 suicides per 100,000 people in the general population.
- Non-Hispanic white men age 85 or older had an even higher rate, with 47 suicide deaths per 100,000.

- Centers for Disease Control and Prevention, National Center for Injury Prevention and Control. Web-based Injury Statistics Query and Reporting System (WISQARS): *www.cdc.gov/ncipc/wisqars*

Fortunately, rather than dwell on his losses, he focused on what he could still do. Doing geriatric assessments has taught me that the elderly do not respond like one might think to the following question: "Do you think your life is useless as it is now?" Geriatric clients usually state that their lives have purpose.

A wonderful teacher, Dr. Carroll Freeman, once stated, "The older people get, the more like themselves they become." He explained that we get good at whatever it is we practice. Gregarious thirty-year-olds become gregarious elderly people. A lifetime of practice leads to mastery. Some of the disagreeableness attributed to the elderly is not an effect of aging, but rather, "perfected" behavior.

Some elderly people have mastered fun, grace, tolerance, and patience. Most people sixty-five years and older are exemplary role models. They are informed, active voters who obey laws, participate in religious services, and contribute their time and financial resources to help others.

We discussed ways to engage her grandfather, including:

Talking:
Always face the elder adult.
Look at him, and unlike football coaches, don't keep the play-by-plays a secret.
Keep obstructions away from your mouth.
Move your lips.
Speak up.
Stand or sit close.
Turn background distractions (television, music, etc.) off.
Be seen.

23

Be heard.

Questioning:
Wait for his response.
Before interrupting with another question or volunteering comment, let him answer.
While you are waiting for him to formulate his response, look at him.
Smile.
Show an interest in hearing him speak.
Include him in conversations.
Ask him what he thinks.

Appointments:
Schedule for mornings.
Before you go, review questions with him. Write questions down.
Practice the responses he might hear.

Driving:
When he cannot or does not want to drive his car, volunteer to drive his car for him.
Let him tell you how it's done and where to go.
So that he knows that you've heard him, repeat aloud what he says.
For departures and arrivals, plan for an extra thirty minutes or more each way. He needs time to gather his cane, glasses, and hat. He also needs to hear, "It's okay; no rush, we've got time."

Remembering:
Try to connect new information to something familiar to him. Before cell phones, people had party lines. Therefore, you might explain that "call waiting" is like a party line without the operator.

Humility:
Let him teach you something his life experience has made him
an expert at. Ask him, "How did you manage."

Changes:
Inform him ahead of time about anticipated changes.
Let him know the plan for his care. If something were to happen
to you, he needs to know who will take care of him.

Lighten up:
Say, "It's okay, Grandpa; we've been lost here before."

The elderly are especially vulnerable in therapy. Their
generation was taught to "manage." If they go to therapy, they
need reassurance that they are not doing something wrong.

9

EXTRAMARITAL COUNSELING

My cousin, Terry, is a private investigator and says that extramarital affairs typically last two years. She has seen, through her specially selected lens, that infatuations plateau and infidelities pain.

A husband made an appointment for couples therapy, which usually means that the marriage is deeply troubled. Comparing calls to schedule therapy to a house fire, a woman will call at the first hint of smoke, whereas a man will be standing in the last smoldering embers of his home and say, "We might need to call somebody." This couple each came to therapy overtly attentive to the other. For a portion of the first session, I saw them separately and learned that he wanted to divorce his wife and had made the appointment to meet me, so he would have the assurance that she was in therapy when he broke the news. Engulfed in the passion of an affair, he could see no other way out. We talked.

Some men will marry "the other woman" because they want to make things right or the other woman is threatening to cut off the relationship, and engulfed in passion, he can't give her up.

In our second session, the husband decided to tell his wife that he wanted a divorce. This was an unusual husband. Most men force the issue—leave clues so their wives will confront them, decide for them. He cleared his throat and told his wife. She knew; she said so with her eyes. Aloud, she protested. Physically, she turned away from him and examined her ring.

Should they separate? They were similar in age, education, politics, religion, geography, had built a marital history, and had binding interests.

What led to the affair? Anger? Lust? Friendship that got out of hand? Had his wife pushed him into an affair? Had she wanted him to cheat, so she could find a way out herself?

What seemed clear is that the husband seemed remorseful. The other woman had flattered him, appreciated him, been there. His wife told me without him in session, I think to protect him, "You know, he, was never an attractive man."

Infidelity is the stated cause for many divorces. Like Angie Dickinson said in an interview, "I divorced my husband because the tabloids told everyone about his affair; I was embarrassed and thought I had to divorce him. That wasn't good enough reason; I loved him."

After their divorces (the other woman divorced also), this particular man disengaged from the community. He and his first wife had built a business. His younger second wife and her children run this business. He became a shadow of himself there and in the community.

When his ex-wife passed away, he called for a session; he wanted to talk about her, about them. When he left her, he lost history. Things had happened, even the affair, and he had wanted to talk to her about it all. She wasn't there any longer to help him with his recall of events, places, and people they had known. He missed his first wife and learned in their separation the value of her presence. But while he had the chance, he couldn't go back, couldn't be wrong a second time. He didn't have the energy.

27

Couples can be too sure that their love will always be. How do couples have lasting love? Unless people are doomed to enter into and repeat tumultuous two-year relationships, they need to recognize that sustaining love requires effort.

Physically, around us we see the second law of thermodynamics at work. Simply stated, everything goes from a state of order to disorder. Most of us routinely purchase warranty agreements and maintenance contracts; the indication is that we are convinced that things will break down. We don't appear too disturbed about having cars repaired, houses repainted, or all the other things we do to in keeping up with our stuff. We responsibly attend to these needs or face the consequences of our inattention.

We erroneously assume that relationships are different. They start out in an orderly fashion, plans are made, couples go on dates, get engaged, get married. Some studies indicate that the more elaborate the wedding, the shorter the marriage. Perhaps, for some couples, the celebration is taken more seriously than is the ceremony.

What, then, is the work of love? Cultivate your common ground. Make a history and celebrate it. Plan weekly play dates, surprises. In your workplace, prominently display photographs (fewer than six months old) of the two of you having fun.

Remember to speak respectfully to and about your mate. Have friends who are good for your marriage who serve as outer barriers of support. Don't be an "artificial single"; most of the time when you go out, go out together.

My uncle Bill and aunt Lou had only one car. They could have had others, but Uncle Bill said that having one car kept him and Aunt Low going in the same direction. They were clearly friends. The right kind of love exclusively honors and holds. I read in I Corinthians 13:13 that love is greater than faith and hope. Faith can move mountains. Imagine the power of l o v e.

10

FATHERING

More women than men go to therapy. Men tend to self-medicate and negate their need for support, therapeutic or otherwise. Their discussing feelings is awkward. When ill, for example, men may ponder aloud, "I think I might be feeling sick." Men will come to therapy though to save their jobs, save their marriages, and a rare man because he wants to save his children.

A single father came to therapy, seemingly too tired to talk. I waited until he had settled in and watched him noticing little around him. Finally, he spoke. "I'm afraid that I'm losing my son, and my ex wants more alimony. Someone at work told me that you helped him, so here I am."

Looking at his weariness, I thought of something Winston Churchill wrote: "It is not enough to say that we are doing our best. We must succeed in doing what is necessary."

This father was taking measured, simple, positive steps to continue. Getting up, putting his shoes on, going to work, and talking to his son were simple, positive acts of courage.

He was in the solitary place of waiting for his child to return to good sense, and his grief was immense. I pointed out that talking while doing something together usually makes it easier for males to bond. This father considered what to do and made a plan to save his child.

He invited his son to take a trip to the Grand Canyon, a place that they had previously visited, which held good recollections for them. He also gave his son the option of visiting a neutral place that, in the past, he had mentioned wanting to see.

He invited his son to spend time with him every week, doing pleasurable things that required some thought: kite-flying; learning how to swing a golf club; building and maintaining a rock, butterfly, vegetable, or flower garden.

They visited university campuses and talked to students from various disciplines who were enthusiastic about their studies.

They took classes, joined clubs, and did community service projects, which broadened both their peer groups.

This dad connected his son to a larger world than the one he had narrowed his interests to. They grew to have a better understanding of each other. Both recognized, each in his own way, that possessions are not substitutes for presence.

This father took the tougher way than many. He tried and found a way to connect. I think they started out on thin ice and moved on to gaining common ground. The son eventually asked his dad to attend a heavy metal concert with him, and the dad went and has the T-shirt.

~11~

FRIENDSHIP

I see a few lonely people in therapy. Seeing a therapist is, for some, the beginning of connecting to another person. The art of the therapeutic relationship is for the therapist to (1) offer support without creating dependency and (2) foster the client's capacity to create a support system outside of therapy sessions.

Fewer and fewer people live and die in the same community where they were born. The distances people live from their families of origin make relatives inaccessible for routine gatherings or babysitting. Friends are critical to support systems.

In their quest for individuality some people grow fragmented and isolated. People do need people; friendships enhance mental health. Given the need that people have to relate, friends take on the roles of extended family members.

Not only do friendships foster mental health, they also boost the immune system. Being with others makes one less likely to succumb to disease.

Relationships are life support. Places to discover friends are: work and work-associated activities, professional organizations, civic groups, church classes, and volunteering.

Seeking friendship carries the potential risk of rejection. In therapy, I give homework assignments to toughen people to this likelihood.

Variations and gradations of this "get rejected" homework assignment are: Go to a mall. As you walk through the mall, hold your head up; smile broadly at every person you see, and count how many people do not return the smile. Next, call ten casual acquaintances and invite them to meet you for coffee or lunch. Go to seven worship services and ask if you may sit on a pew where others are already seated.

Being a friend means being friendly and sometimes vulnerable. True friends hold each other accountable and don't let you get away with things "on the down low," or as I prefer to say, "low down."

As critical as friendships are to wellness, I believe that no one person can fully satisfy another. If human beings could be complete with other people, no need for God would exist. Friendships do have limitations, but they are a great contributor to overall well-being. When we were born, our families brought community to us. As adults, we have the opportunity and personal responsibility to create families, communities of our own choosing.

Therapy is a safe place to begin building rapport with another person. I ask clients to show me how to look when approaching another person. If I want someone to talk to me, what are my teeth doing? Grimacing? Ready to bite? We do role plays; wherein I look down and mumble. Clients demonstrate how to correct myself. I get "defensive" saying, "Whadda ya mean you couldn't hear me?" So! I talk to my feet!

The longer a person lives, the fewer friends he may have; friendship attrition happens; people are lost through death, misunderstandings, moves, and retirement. Establishing, building, and restoring friendships are life enhancements for mental and physical health. **Lone**ly not. I strongly encourage clients to develop and work at maintaining friendships.

~12~

GRATITUDE

An altered state of mind may be accomplished through twirling around and around. Rethinking too can change a heart. As this hymnist wrote:

> When upon life's billows you are tempest tossed,
> When you are discouraged, thinking all is lost,
> Count your many blessings, name them one by one,
> And it will surprise you what the Lord hath done.
> —Johnson Oatman, Jr. 1856-1922

This is an account of something I learned from a child who was visiting and having a snack. She asked for seconds, and as I handed her the second treat, I asked, "What do you say?"

The child concentrated, looked up at me and said, with some hesitation, "More?"

Certainly, she was appreciative and wanted more of the good treatment I was offering her but seemed unfamiliar with expressing gratitude. She was confident of good things to come and trusted me to follow through, and I did.

35

I laughed at her, then at myself, seeing the picture of myself through her behaving in the same way. I so often go to God seeking His hands, something from Him, rather than His face, relationship.

Expressing gratitude for both what we have and the many things we have been spared can be learned and provides a plethora of benefits.

Bowing our heads to pray, focus then say . . . thank you. Two, four, six, eight, who do we appreciate? Reminds us.

The advantages of expressing gratitude are manifold. Spouses who take the time to say aloud what they appreciate about the other get more of the same. People attending to positives report that their lives are happier than in times past when they negated, minimized, or ignored the good in their lives.

In a multitude of languages and images, I encourage you to make a visual collage of happy: occasions, people, places, and things immersed throughout with these words, thank you.

~13~

HOLIDAY SHOULDS

A wife said that she would not be putting up any decorations. Her husband usually left her a few weeks before Christmas, and she had learned that the festivities were just too much for him. She said he couldn't deal with putting up a tree.

Holidays bring music of the season, shopping, and extra helpings of opportunities for gatherings of people. From the polished commercials we see, it seems apparent that people smile, food is passed about, people wear their best, people wrap packages and sing carols to people whom they seldom see who seem remarkably glad to see them. The message, too, seems to be that events and gatherings need to be presented and received in a prescribed manner.

This expectation may bring a burden of "shoulds." A symmetrical table setting a must, and for the full effect, people seated according to weight and height. Each person must have an equal number of equally priced gifts, and won't it be awful if they don't! People will quit crying and smile for photographs. The lists endless and undoubtedly checked twice.

Families are a blend of individuals who may or may not have the same ideas about how to celebrate the season. Tolerance for these differences and embracing the different forms of celebration may enrich the whole experience. The significance of the celebration is not a substitute for the importance of the family's comfort. Some people are a family of one and need not feel discomforted.

Distress may be a mild or disturbing distraction. During the holidays, despondency and depression can be exacerbated by the unrealistic, unattainable goals that many media (television shows, movies, songs, programs, family traditions) set for us.

Should the cookies be dry, the batteries for the camera be lost or dead, the perfect gift be the wrong color, Aunt Jenny forget herself and spill her eggnog? Should these things happen? Yes. In real life, unless the event is rehearsed and a camera crew available to get each person's placement staged, unexpected turns and spills will happen.

Should everything and everyone be picture-perfect? Then it is a photograph—untouchable and un-huggable. Yes, it would be pleasant if the cookies were moist, the batteries in the camera fresh, givers of gifts appreciated, Aunt Jenny didn't have Alzheimer's disease, table settings were symmetrical, and people didn't cry at Christmas.

This couple let go of pressuring people and things to be a certain way. This spouse created an oasis of quiet and gave the gift of peace.

14

HURRICANE KATRINA

In August 2005, Hurricane Katrina destroyed and disillusioned more than can be numerated. Families were both scattered to parts before unseen and gathered in places they would never have believed possible. Ex-spouses and mates were forced to take shelter under the same roof.

Routine therapy sessions were out, so I did sessions in what people had left of their homes. I heard repeatedly, I lost everything; I have nothing left." But, internet searches and calls to radio station WWL were from people looking for people, not material possessions.

Couples exercised faith, hope, and love anew. They exercised faith in believing that the members of their families that they could not find were making every effort to be safe and found. They exercised hope in believing that things would get better. Their love for each other was their super glue.

What couples who stayed together found was that Hurricane Katrina did not destroy their capacity for renewal. They had left exactly what they needed: faith, hope, and love, and like any exercise, exertion caused new awareness of areas that needed support, practice, or a spotter. They ached all over.

Couples who did not make it through Katrina as partners were overwhelmingly angry at their circumstances, at Federal Emergency Management Agency (FEMA), at their spouses, and themselves. Men in particular felt they had let their families down. The sentiment was not logical but definitely heartfelt. They were "supposed to" hold back the hurricane-force winds and keep the water out.

What helped was a sense of empowerment over some small aspect, like finding a place to wash clothes. Then came control over greater parts of their lives, like finding a reputable contractor.

The stages of denial, anger, bargaining, depression, and acceptance, defined by Dr. Elizabeth Kubler-Ross for the terminally ill and their families, help explain the impact of losses. The process is not tidy, with one stage neatly done and then progress to the next stage, but concentric, with stages overlapping others.

During Katrina and for months and years afterward, clients refer to defining moments associated with the event. Some people came to therapy for the first time, and others are just starting to talk about their experiences.

15

JEALOUS

One of my clients presented with an issue not her own. She could be happy only when she was certain that others were not as well off. I said as convincingly as I could, "Yes, I can see how unhappy you must be to know that your life is so much worse than everyone else's life. You are the most unattractive and the poorest person in the community."

She countered with, "That's not true. I am happy, and I *am* attractive and rich!"

To this, I replied, "Oh, I don't understand then."

Gregory Bateson wrote, "That which is good for us taken to excess becomes toxic."

Sleeping and eating are critical functions for well-being. Yet too much of either can create ill health.

Toxicity may manifest itself other ways too. Socially, demonstrating an honest, open, sincere admiration of others' possessions and giving compliments is unselfish.

Some individuals lose balance, and what may have begun as an appreciation for another's assets may grow to be a toxic, jealous obsession.

At the least, jealousy may become a source of discontentment, and at its worst, a precipitating factor in violating social constraints and committing crimes.

People with this tendency appear to feel that they have been deprived and are somehow entitled to take what others have. People who are jealous often internalize their obsessions, personalizing their beliefs in three ways. 1. They imagine that people who have what they want to possess are affronting them on purpose. 2. They feel that people who have what they want have deprived them. 3. To empowering themselves, they try to take from others.

These actions may be obvious or hidden. In what seems to be an inconsequential manner, they may belittle the person or the possessions of those whom they feel have deprived them and may feel entitled to steal from these "withholding" others.

The depth of their toxicity is revealed in how these attempts of "repossession" fail to gratify. Unrepentant for their actions against others and unsatisfied, they continue to seek some greater asset to consume.

Jealousy causes people to move *against* people. Appreciation causes people to move *toward* people.

People I see in therapy are sometimes there because of toxicity inflicted upon them by others.

In explaining herself to me, this client began to see that her unhappiness was essentially self-inflicted. She took nine months to explain it. She gave birth to a new identity, one self composed and not so inclined to be overpowered by jealousy.

~16~

MILITARY

I understand some of the distresses of military personnel and their families. I recall my own anxiety about my dad leaving to go to Saudi Arabia and my mother's tears when he wasn't home. I hold these thoughts to myself as I listen.

A man came to session. His handshake strong, his eyes bewildered. He was there because his second wife had just moved out, and his business associates were distancing themselves from him. He said, "I have AA issues."

I said, "You're in AA?"

Client: "No, I have problems with anxiety and anger, AA."

Me: "On a scale of one to ten, one being barely anxious and ten being the most anxious you've ever been, how are you feeling right now?"

Client: "Seven."

Me: "And anger?"

Client: "About a five."

"Tell me the last time you were angry."

Client: "Three weeks ago, my son left his bicycle in the driveway, and my wife didn't think it was that big a deal."

Me: "Who were you more angry with, your son or your wife?"

Client: "My wife!"

It seemed best not to comment and exaggerate the obvious; he was still angry. Years back in therapy, couples who were angry were given foam bats and encouraged to hit each other. Six months later, couples were angrier than when they started.

Me: "She didn't take your side."

Client: "She didn't even get upset about it."

Me: "You felt like she disregarded the importance of what happened? Then, when you got angry, you felt disrespected."

Client: "Yes, I blew up."

Me: "In the past, when you blew things up, you were given medals. But now, blowing up doesn't make things safer. And you want to learn how to control it, stay safe?"

Client: "Yes."

Me: "And you're getting anxious about feeling anxious, which makes you feel more anxious?"

Then he talked for thirty minutes, his speech growing less pressured, quieter.

Me: "I think controlling your anger will resolve some of your anxiety issue. You have the discipline from your military training to follow through with the orders I'm giving you. Practice one or two of these things.

Me: "When you feel the anger beginning, you hear your voice change, feel your blood starting to gush; pause and think of your daughter's name and spell it backward. Imagine yourself stepping up to be awarded a medal for bravery in getting along with civilians, The Soldier Who Knows Best How to Calm Himself Medal of Bravery. Physically tug on your earlobe and ground yourself. Think of ten places in the world that you think are beautiful, and hold each place in your mind's eye for two-seconds. Breathe in slowly to the count of four, hold this breath two-seconds, to the count of four, and let your breath out. Repeat four times. Carry a rock in your pocket, and when the anger starts, hold the rock in your hand as though it is a small, small you; and promise yourself that this rock, has nothing to fear from you. Take a moment, separate yourself from the situation."

Me: "Do this one now. Tense your whole body, from curling your toes to grimacing your face, and hold this fierce tension for thirty-seconds, and then, in five-second segments, let the tension go."

Client: "Okay, Doc. I can't believe I feel better."

Me: "How's your anger?"

Client: "Two."

Me: "Anxiety?"

Client: "One."

MOTHERING

A young woman told me, "Time has run out on me. I'll never be a mother now." Yes, I agreed, biologically this would be her case. The grief associated with maternal loss is deep and difficult for others to understand. It's not that she regretted that others were mothers; rather, she was saddened that she would not be. I listened to what she said and paid close attention to what she *didn't* say. She didn't talk about children past infancy, so I brought that up.

Women may become mothers without birthing their young. Mothers rear children and seek to make the best impressions. Plato wrote, "Do you not know, then, that the beginning in every task is the chief thing, especially for any creature that is young and tender? For it is then that it is best molded and takes the impression that one wishes to stamp upon it."

Constant, steady, strong presence makes a firm imprint. Taught and caught lessons help or hinder children throughout life. Mothers set limits, work hard to make correct impressions, and hold at bay harmful experiences from which they want to protect their young.

Guarantees of productive outcomes do not exist, and good mothering does not equal "good" children. Mothers give their stamp of approval for good behavior; children, however, make choices of their own. All influences leave marks.

Given the life lessons that mothers model, it is imperative that children spend time with their mothers. Imprints may be made in atypical ways. For instance, know your child's schedule, and occasionally, on a humdrum school day, make a surprise visit. Sign your student out, saying that she has an appointment. Take the child to an early lunch or a fun movie. Not knowing when Mom may drop by gives the student a sense of seriousness about completing school assignments and something happy to anticipate.

Despite a mother's effort, a child may see or hear something that she very much wanted to keep from him; however, the strength of her presence and talking about the images may temper the impact of the experience.

What a child needs to know is that he is valuable—especially when he feels least deserving. Knowing that Mom has expectations is a compliment. The child may grasp her faith and believe that he is capable.

Mothers, like their children, are not perfect. Children learn from hearing their mothers admit, "I blew it; I'm sorry. Please forgive me. I overreacted." Mothering is a lifelong job; the love poured into this work, boundless. Years after children leave home, when life skins their knees, they want Mom to make it better.

This client explored her own life experience and numerated the other women who had mothered her and discovered that her gifts of good health, monetary independence, and time were definite assets to mothering the children of others in her life. Mothering and prayer are natural cohabiters. She's become the prayerful voice for parents and the confidant, the objective, available ear to her nieces and nephews.

~18~

NEARLY BELOVED

A man came in for a session and seemed to me too eager to please, too accommodating. He said his wife had committed adultery, and he was trying to adjust. In our second session, I purposefully moved the office furniture so that he would be sitting with the glare of the sun in his eyes. He sat for twenty minutes, trying to shield his eyes and adjust his posture away from the glare. I watched his discomfort, hoping that he would make a move. Finally, he asked to move! I applauded that assertive baby step he took in voicing his needs.

He had miles to go, still ahead of him. The problem of being alone is that nobody is there. He would have to decide how he would manage himself without her. Everyone is born single; adults, though, fall into three categories: single, married, and single again (widowed, divorced, or separated).

Some forms of service may best be done as a single. **Single:** Mother Teresa of Calcutta (1910-1997). As a Missionary of Charity, she took upon herself and embodied four vows: poverty, chastity, obedience, and a pledge of service to the poor. Her life's ministry was to serve the sick. In 1979, she was awarded the Nobel Peace Prize.

Starting out single is a familiar place when single again. **Single, married, single again:** C.S. Lewis (1898-1963), professor at Oxford and Cambridge, wrote works including *The Lion, the Witch and the Wardrobe*; *The Problem of Pain;* volumes of Broadcast Talks from his radio lectures for the BBC; and my favorite of his writings, *The Screwtape Letters.* Lewis did marry at fifty-eight years of age and was married for three years until his wife, Joy, died in 1960.

Single, married: Louis Pasteur (1822-1895), chemist and biologist, countered the accepted theory of the Academy of Medicine, which espoused that illness grew within the individual and not from an outside source. Pasteur sought to prove that germs caused disease. He researched to find and kill these microbes. What is his legacy? We wash our hands. Milk is pasteurized. The world has vaccines. Medical procedures include sterilization. Pasteur's family also sacrificed their time with him.

I recall an elderly, single missionary's answer to "Didn't you want to marry and have children?"

She said in her rather scratchy but stately voice, "Yes, and I asked God to send someone to me. God sent him, but he did not come."

One can love wholly, and this is what the gentleman who came to see me learned to do, first for himself. The glare of the sun in his eyes that day and his reaction seemed to light his soul in understanding. He sensed his discomfort, made a statement, took a stand, and made a move. He learned to embrace himself.

~19~

OBSESSION

A young man came to session, so preoccupied with a former mate that he thought he was losing his mind. He couldn't concentrate on work or even read. He wanted to forget her, forget *them*, but he kept being reminded of their every experience. She was locked into his sensory memory—intruding on her touch, smell, presence, voice, and taste.

I didn't try to remove her. I asked him if he was willing to do whatever I asked him to do for five days and have another session. Then I would explain my reasoning.

He was miserable and lost; he said, "Yes."

I asked him what time he usually woke up, and he said 6:00 a.m.

I gave him the following assignment. Every morning for the next five days, set your alarm for 4:00 a.m. Then get up, sit in a chair, and think about her. Give your mind no prohibition at all in what you think. Then, at 5:00 am, stop. For the remainder of the day, whenever she comes to mind, remind yourself that you have a 4:00 a.m. appointment and will think only of her then.

An hour after our session, I called him and said, "It is not unusual to feel exposed after a first disclosure. Call if you need to talk before our next session." After the first session, I call clients to follow up, to check on them and reassure them that I heard them.

In five days, he returned, clean-shaven, hair combed, non-bleary-eyed. I knew without his saying so that he had kept his 4:00 a.m. appointments.

The reasoning, of course, was for him to recognize that he had control over his own thought processes. Controlling his obsession defused its power.

I saw him every week for six weeks in a row, then every other week, at three-week intervals, then monthly, and bimonthly.

He was baffled by his ex-mate's behavior. He genuinely loved her, missed them. He suffered, but from that first session on, he suffered less and less.

He was able to gain objectivity and accept her choices without personalizing it and recognize that neither he nor she was all good or all bad.

The 4:00 a.m. appointment was meant to be inconvenient. Into the third week, he couldn't sit through an hour of just thinking about her and began skipping the 4:00 a.m. appointments. Sitting in a chair was to ensure that he would be alert but not active. Movement would have released endorphins, the feel-good, pain-inhibiting hormones. Initially, I wanted him to associate some physical discomfort with thoughts of her and empower himself to dissociate from the unpleasantness.

One reason people in argumentative, physically abusive relationships repeat the cycle is the release of endorphins during their conflicts. His thoughts of her at 4:00 am allowed no such release.

~20~

PANIC

A caterer, Jim, called me in the middle of a wedding reception, saying, "Doc, I'm having a panic attack!"

I said, "Walk to the bathroom and let me hear you breathing aloud with me." He did. In ninety-seconds, he was calm.

Then we talked. I asked if someone could work instead of him, and he said no.

Of course, no one could take over for him; he thinks he's indispensable and indestructible. I know him.

Me: "Is your wife there?"

Client: "Yes, she's stirring a pot of gumbo."

Me: "Here's what I want you to do: in the next two hours, if you feel yourself panicking, stop whatever you are doing, and go to your wife and kiss her passionately."

He laughed.

Panic attacks last three to five minutes. Distractions help ease the discomfort. Some people simply count the seconds until the panic attack is over. Wearing an elastic band on the wrist and snapping it causes pain. Breathing into a paper bag helps visualize breathing. Focus on some stationary object. Count the number of tiles in the ceiling or floor. Sing badly.

"Also," I said, "tonight if you feel it necessary but definitely in the morning, call your MD and have your heart tested. Get a signed release of your tests, and bring me the results."

Stress responses are necessary. Survival depends on the stress response. So blood may be directed to the muscles and the brain, and digestion slows. Ever feel butterflies in your stomach? To supply more oxygen to the muscles, breathing speeds up. Recall trying to catch your breath after being frightened? The heart rate gets faster, and blood pressure soars, forcing blood to the parts of the body that need it. After you are suddenly forced to stop in traffic, feel your heart pounding. To cool the body, perspiration increases. Commercials to sell deodorant remind us of this action. The muscles tense. After a stressful meeting, ever have a backache or stiff neck? To make the blood clot more quickly, chemicals are released. For quick energy, sugars and fats pour into the bloodstream. Cortisol is secreted. In dangerous situations, these responses keep us alive. Routinely making these responses, however, causes extra wear and tear on the organs.

After all physical maladies were ruled out, I advised Jim to take measures to manage his stress responses: listening to music he enjoys, hearing funny stories, breathing deeply, walking in a measured, steady manner.

I asked Jim to think of the particular situation of his "emergency" in the context of the whole. He has a successful catering business, and that is why his work is in demand. Were he mediocre, he wouldn't have so many customers.

His anxiety was usually helpful and kept him from being overconfident or complacent. This anxiety, however, was different; it paralyzed him and gave cause for him to imagine he was having a heart attack.

He was able to restore his confidence in his capacity to continue his business. After the medical clearance session, I asked him to take a short vacation, and he did go—eventually. His first vacation in three years. I think my complimenting him about the substantial estate his passing would bring his attractive wife was the clincher.

He is industrious and tenacious and finds it hard to take time off. To wean himself from working too many hours and days, I suggested he take breaks of a few hours, then a day, and then another day.

What he learned is that the change of scenery made him better able to enjoy his work and have a fresh perspective. When he is away and panic sets in, he repeats, "I love my life. I love my life. I love my life."

Seeing friends for therapy is not my usual practice. Definite boundaries have to be maintained and no room left for misinterpretation for compromise. I charge Jim the same rate as everyone else, and he cuts me no slack on catering.

~21~

PREMARITAL COUNSELING

In sessions for engaged couples, I have one session take the form of a dating game. Couples discover the other's expectations. Couples taking the narrow path of premarital counseling need not worry that they will learn too much to soon.

Day-to-day and night-to-night living together allows many times to say "I do" or "I don't" and "we do" or "we don't."

Seven C's:

Communication: In this regard, you might think that couples today have a great advantage over past generations. The means of connecting seem endless: e-mails, texting, chats, video, calls from anywhere. These forms of messaging are good but are not a substitute for what couples in love want to do: be with their mates in real time. Couples, for a lifetime, guard against sharps. They avoid cutting each other off or cutting each other down to size. They listen and enter into the other's world and hunger to be wherever the other is. Away from their mates, they take note of what they will share with that exceptional other.

Change: Successful couples make agreements about how to manage their money and set limits about spending. For any purchase outside the amounts they have decided to spend without the other's presence, they wait until check in.

Cooking: At home or out, they use meals to explore tastes and experience senses anew. They share bites and savor flavors, learning what the other likes cultivating an appreciation for the other's tastes.

Children: If children become part of the relationship, they recognize that children share in the wealth and reserves of their love. Weekly date nights are crucial, and children can learn to delight and have security in their parents' dressing up to meet each other.

Couple: They may *spend time* with others, but they *share significant events* together. They create their own traditions and may include others. They do not often allow themselves to be seen without the other. They don't allow themselves to become viewed as single. When one is without the other, talk of their beloved is effortless. One has the sense that the other is missed. They carry recent pictures.

Communion: They honor faith traditions and call upon spiritual support to sustain goodwill and withstand distresses.

Confirmation: They affirm each other sexually.
Premarital counseling is important to nurturing growth in intimacies.

~22~

SMOKIN'

Patients who smoke are usually doing so as a coping mechanism. I recall doing an assessment on a patient and writing only the word *smokes* in the section for coping mechanisms. The individual doing the medical assessment was incensed. I recall explaining, "I didn't say it was a healthy strategy, but I do believe that this patient smokes to cope."

Cigarette smoking and other forms of tobacco used to be promoted and embraced. Men smoked and women dipped snuff.

When I was growing up, I never heard concerns about first or secondhand smoke. My parents both smoked. Between the two of them, they puffed four to six packs of cigarettes a day. Gasps and gagging preceded their morning awakening.

Mom and Dad's smoking was a constant for all events: christenings, weddings, funerals, graduations, holidays. Before they left the house, they made sure they had an adequate supply of cigarettes and lighters. I guess some of their friends did not smoke, though at the time, it seemed that every adult I knew smoked.

We children were too young to smoke, so we bought candy "cigarettes." Opening the packs released a wispy cloud of dust and left a residue of white film on our hands. The red-painted tip gave this candy the look of the real deal. We mimicked the adults we saw at home and in the movies. We tried to hold them "just right." The candy did not last long in our hands; we invariably nibbled the sticks away. We shook them from the pack, shared them with each other, and "smoked" whole packs in minutes.

My mother quit smoking about three times a year: on Ash Wednesday for the forty days of Lent, New Year's Day, and some other time of personal significance to her. In between these periods of abstinence, she talked about giving it up for good. Ingenious in her attempts, she took up the pipe and used filters—longer and longer filters. She died a smoker.

My father never looked movie star macho with a cigarette. In his huge hands, cigarettes looked like comical aberrations. After his heart attack, however, Dad quit smoking.

In the past twenty years, movie stars have quit smoking on screen, and around the world, children are "smoking" fewer cigarette-looking candies. Many smokers say they want to quit smoking. And, according to Mark Twain, it's easy; he said he knew because he had given it up many times.

Psychological addiction to smoking is harder to conquer than the physiological addiction. Seneca wrote, "It is part of the cure to wish to be cured." Smokers may practice purposeful avoidance of places and situations that trigger cues to smoke. Keep hands busy. My Dad took up crossword puzzles. Patches, chewing gum, medications, and meditation may help. Some smokers quit often. The more often a smoker quits, the closer the quitting episodes get to each other, which increases the likelihood that he may become a total quitter. Smoking cessation is one activity wherein society accepts and applauds a quitter.

~23~

SUPPORT

People see therapists to be heard, but the words may not come easy. Clients arriving for their first sessions are typically nervous. While waiting, they cross and uncross their arms and their legs. They pace. They sit down. They stand up again. When I see them, I ask, "What brings you in today?"

Their first responses are often noncommittal; they are testing the waters. Their discomfort may be unspeakable, so I ask two defining questions. First: "Why did you make the appointment now?"

A young adult might make an appointment with me because he is going through his first failed class and doesn't know how he will tell his family. A wife might make an appointment because her husband's affairs have encroached upon her friendships. Some call because they are ready to make healthy changes or get a psychological tune-up.

My second question: "When things are what you want them to be, how will you know?" In other words, when you wake up in the morning, what will you hear and see?

A child in a family session said with certainty, "I'll know things are okay again when I wake up and smell breakfast cooking!" He went on to describe the morning and how the whole day would go.

I ask these questions to define therapeutic outcomes and understand how we will satisfy a client's expectations. When clients define what they want aloud, they are often surprised to learn that they have some of the answer already in place. They learn the exceptions to the problem. Like, my child doesn't leave a mess at my mom's house but leaves food everywhere at home. I say, please describe how mealtimes differ at your mom's house. Client responds, at her house, they eat at the table; at home, he eats alone in front of the television . . .

~24~

TALK

This is a personal account that, for me, underscores the value of talking aloud. After my mother's cataract surgery, we went to her doctor's office to have her bandages removed. When we got there, I saw twenty-five or more individuals in the waiting room, half of whom were wearing bandages over one or both eyes. I saw patients groping their way into the room and feeling their way into chairs for certainty that they were truly sitting down in the right place. Other than my mom, I didn't know another person in the place.

I directed a question at the lady sitting on my left. But due to the faulty eyesight of half the people present, I was answered by about a dozen people, which sent what had been a silent waiting room into a buzz of talk. I asked, "What happened to your eye?"

Their responses were immediate; I was surprised. Into the next hour, elderly people talked about what happened to their eyes—cataract surgeries, cornea scratches, what happened in their lives leading up to their surgeries. They talked in my general direction and got acquainted with each other. Some showed, the best they could, pictures from their purses and wallets.

Driving my mom home, I asked myself, *What happened in that waiting room?* Their stoic silence and the subsequent flurry of words astonished me. I am used to clients telling me what happened, but a whole group of strangers talking was healing too. These patients had a common experience, which had just happened to them. Their words seemed pent up, and they seemed relieved to release them. I think, in some way, their talking relieved them of a burden. They learned that they were not alone in having to keep up their onerous schedules of applying eye drops and seeing to eye care. They came to know that others were also having trouble keeping their balance. They found out that others in that waiting room were struggling to find their place. They talked about their experiences and gotten better and gave each other the hope of recovery.

Discovering that their seemingly unusual reactions to eye surgery were ordinary experiences allowed them sighs of relief and laughter.

Talking heals. I am supposed to know that, however, seeing mere talking help in an unexpected setting, at an unexpected time, renewed my belief in the impact and power of saying the words aloud that reverberate in the silence of one's mind.

~25~

THE SIMPLE LIFE

A couple came to session, not to talk about their sex life—often the covert reason why couples schedule an appointment—but to talk through their disagreement about the accumulation of material things.

A rule in therapy is if it ain't broke, don't fix it. For example, some couples refer to each other as Mommy and Daddy, and frankly that seems peculiar to me, but if that isn't why they called, I don't explore it.

I asked each of them pointed questions, and the other "overheard" the other talk. They discovered. The wife wanted a smaller house, and the husband wanted a larger boat. They were caught between the strain of simplifying their lives and accumulating more.

Their tug of war is common. Sellers do not typically encourage buyers to wait, reflect, or discuss transactions. Pressures confront people to make immediate, spur-of-the-moment buys. Marketing schemes imply that if you have this thing, you will be complete;

people will like you; you will belong; you will be safe. These messages strike deep into the psyche.

Items bought may symbolize another need. It is true that a man wanting a larger boat may be trying to compensate for a small penis; it is also true that his size may require a more substantial seating area.

What this couple learned is that they were equally anxious about losing something meaningful to them. For him, letting go of some extras provoked anxiety. The cushion of having things around comforted him. To feel better, he had only to look around to see things. Buying things gave him relief. Material possessions reminded him of prosperity and distanced him from scarcity. Fewer possessions made him feel vulnerable and exposed. He couldn't understand his wife's unappreciative attitude, and she couldn't get his distancing himself, putting things between them. For her, possessions were worrisome; she felt obligated to tend to upkeep and gave cause for her to enjoy her life less. She felt that she was losing her husband to things. She wanted a smaller house, so she could have him closer by, more often in the same room. They compromised.

After a few sessions, they decided to practice restraint in accumulating and letting go. She recognized that what appeared to her to be extravagance was moderation to her spouse. He learned that his presence was of more value than objects to his wife. He subsequently bought the boat, and she learned to navigate their travels.

For me this couple was ideal. When they learned what mattered to the other, they were respectful of the other's needs and made the effort to compromise.

TIME

A man nearing retirement came to discuss closure issues. "Losing his job" was his choice but difficult. We made a list of the pros and cons. Materially, he was gaining, yet emotionally, he was struggling. The chief issue was time lost. He realized he would not have time left to win the Boston Marathon. Truth was, his job had been a healthy distraction from his aging. Retiring meant that he would be facing losses that were happening for years but left unnoticed. Time hadn't waited for him.

We are not born equal. Some of us are born into love and affluence. Others of us face challenges of birth, which are difficult to overcome.

Time, however, is the area where we are all equal. True, we are granted different numbers of days, but for every day that we live, we are granted twenty-four-hours.

Unlike money, we cannot manage time. If we could manage time, I think somewhere a time bank would exist where minutes and hours from days that linger too long could be deposited and redeemed later. Then we could cash in our time deposits and have the extra hours that we need to meet deadlines and visit with our family and friends.

We cannot collect on time past. Minutes are used—not invested but consumed. Future time, too, is not a guarantee. Human beings have an unknown but certain expiration date. Whether days, months, or years lie ahead of us, we get to that future time by the minute, in the moments that we live.

Too often, in our rush to get to a place we call "then," we wish away time.

When I retire, then . . .
When I graduate, then . . .
When I get the job, then . . .
When I sell the house, then . . .
When I buy the house, then . . .
When the baby is born, then . . .
When the children graduate, then . . .
When the children move out (again), then . . .

Before then, we are in the now. If this moment is difficult, take heart; it won't last forever. If this moment is pleasurable, appreciate it, for it too will not last.

Because time cannot be managed, in the time that we are allotted, we can attempt only to manage ourselves. As we strive to accomplish short—and long-term goals, we may do so with renewed awareness of the time that is ticking away.

This retiree clarified his values, goals and relationships and made plans to be not merely *on* time but *in* time.

We met three more times. I admired his taking notice, admitting that he had been rarely present in his life and determined to "catch" himself from detaching. We did this by developing a code word. He picked a word in common use, and whenever he hears the word, he "checks in" to see if he really is present, listening, participating in the conversation, in life.

A word could be coffee (not the word he is using); every time you hear the word, do a self-check. **Time** (I'm; I am present).

~27~

TRANSITIONS

Client: "I hate it when I wake up and can't remember what I did wrong, *this* time."

Me: "You are troubled about things you do that you feel are wrong?"

Interpreting what a client is feeling is risky. I might misinterpret; when I do, clients usually clarify.

Client: "Isn't killing somebody wrong?"

I gulped and said, "That's hard to hear."

The client said, "I'm joking."

I looked at him, suddenly aware of the hour, and asked myself, *Why am I meeting this stranger so late in the evening?* But, said aloud, Me: "Tell me everything."

He said he was going through a change. Everyone is.

All transitions mean something, someone, someplace left. Talking through transitions is about safely negotiating change and making appropriate adjustments. The longer people wait, the longer the processes take.

Some changes are immediately recognized as loss: dealing with keeping damaging secrets, facing death, divorcing, downsizing, one's home being blown away by hurricanes, and distressing over events of war. Even planned events such as career advances, marriage, moving, parenting, and vacation include giving up other possibilities.

Attending to the details involved in negotiating changes is distracting, and people generally do not directly address their misgivings, especially when their changes have been celebrated. Career advances alter relationships. Marriage requires giving up singleness. Moving to a different house, even in the same neighborhood, involves the loss of something familiar. Parenting erodes personal freedom. Selecting a vacation destination negates all the other possible choices. In the midst of these good happenings, people may feel the vibrations of ill-ease and wonder, *What's wrong with me?*

Others effected by the transition may not be available to hear the acknowledgment, and telling them could give them cause to wonder. They may misinterpret and magnify statements, which you did not mean to be definitive but explored. Squelching these feelings can be fatiguing.

Negating the impact of the adjustments made or minimizing life-changing events, may cause physical illness.

I met with a client on the day he learned that his divorce was final.

Me: "How are you?"

He said jubilantly, "Oh! I couldn't be better."

He had tears in his eyes. When what I hear does not match what I see, I believe my eyes. He was talking to someone not emotionally involved with the situation, yet he took some moments to admit aloud how much he was hurting.

Me: "The tears in your eyes don't look happy."

Client: "What'd you expect?"

Me: "Your mouth is smiling, but your eyes have tears. I was expecting you to be like that, mixed up today.

His mental, and I believe physical well-being were enhanced by attending to his perceptions. Clients talking aloud clarify assessments of themselves and choices they have made.

Getting the words out matters and can be done by praying aloud, recording then listening. Writing thoughts down and reading aloud what is written are helpful exercises.

Therapists and clergy members are useful for this purpose. Someone who will keep confidences is priceless.

UNDER THE INFLUENCE

For years, I taught defensive driving per driver improvement courses to individuals convicted of driving while intoxicated (DWI) and driving under the influence (DUI). The consequences of arrest are severe. All drivers who drink are vulnerable to arrest.

Individuals charged and in my classes have said:

Student: "I don't know why I was arrested; I was asleep."

Me: "Where were you?"

Student: "In my car, on the Interstate."

Student: "I broke up with my boyfriend, and I went out and had a few drinks."

Me: "How many?"

Student: "A few dozen."

Student: "I was set up. The cops know the bars close at 2 a.m., and there they were, just waiting for me. That's entrapment!"

Typically the arrest process starts with the officer stopping the driver for problematic vehicle management. The driver presents his or her driver's license, proof of insurance, and vehicle registration. The officer uses discretion about whether to administer a breathalyzer test, which measures blood alcohol concentration (BAC). Additional assessments may include urine and blood work. Along the side of the road, the driver will be required to do a field sobriety test, which may include reciting some portion of the alphabet, walking a straight line, standing on one foot, and touching one's nose.

Drivers who fail any one of these tests will be read the Miranda warning, arrested, handcuffed, placed in the back seat of a law-enforcement vehicle, taken to jail, and fingerprinted.

Confidentiality is not respected; newspapers list the driver's name, address, and offense. Convictions are public and costly. Costs to the driver include: insurance rate increases, attorney fees, court costs, towing, impoundment fees, and potential lost wages from time served in jail. Additional costs may include termination from work, disqualification from school programs, and ineligibility for work advancements.

Vehicular accidents do happen. No driver is exempt from the possibility. Sober drivers involved in accidents may have the assurance of knowing that alcohol consumption was not an impairment. When alcohol is a factor in an accident, its influence cannot be ruled out. Driving poses risk.

Given the grave consequences, it is imperative that people do not drink and drive. This can be accomplished by the following actions.

If you are home, having a drink, and an argument escalating to violence ensues, call someone to take you to a safe place.

When you go out to drink, leave your vehicle at home.

Give your keys to someone to hold for you.

Plan to stay at a hotel near where you are going out.

Call someone to pick you up and take you home.

Have two designated drivers.

If you are at a friend's house, ask to stay overnight.

Reserve a limousine.

Call a taxi to take you home.

Not all adults drink, and certainly adults who do drink do not drink all the time. When offered an alcoholic drink, people who do not drink or have quit drinking do not have to elaborate and may put others at ease by saying, "Thanks. I'll have a Coke (tea, water)."

~29~

WHEN PARENTS DATE

A client was in therapy for issues related to unresolved grief and seemed not her usual self, so I asked, "What is it that you haven't said that you think I need to hear?"

Without hesitation (but with some reservation), she said, "My mother is acting weird."

Me: "How is that?"

"She seems distracted . . . not interested in eating . . . forgets what I just said."

Me: "What's new with her?"

Client: "She's started seeing a man from her church."

"Sounds like she is in love," I offered.

My client, I think, would have preferred a diagnosis of dementia. Her mother's dating amplified my client's grief.

Until this generation, adult children did not as often have to deal with seeing their parents date. In ages past, a widowed parent might or might not have dated. Now, however, parents live longer, and divorce increases the possibility.

I hear adult children voicing concerns that their own parents presented to me years ago when *they* were dating. It's difficult to know what to do when your parent is seeing someone you find unacceptable, the following actions may help ease anxiety and tension.

Include the person in family gatherings. If you avoid this person's presence, you may force your parent to choose either her family or her boyfriend. Invite him to family gatherings; allow your mom to see him and observe his conversation and interactions with others.

Take a trip with your mom, invite her closest friends and family. Build bridges that allow her to reconnect. Cherish this time. If your mom decides to stay with Mr. What-is-she-thinking, then you will have this trip to recall. Having time away from him will allow her to regain objectivity and garner her resolve to decide for herself. If she decides to marry him, and the marriage proves to be an unfortunate match, she needs to know that she has support.

She needs a prenuptial agreement, but you are probably not the one to tell her. Your broaching this subject may move her toward him in defense of his character and cause her to distance herself from you. Her friends or attorney discussing the prenup may be easier for her to accept.

In time, you may learn that he isn't a villain, but someone respectable and a suitable life mate. While your feelings may be real, they may also not be accurate.

Your parents are the people you may become. Eventually, they will be looking up to you.

~30~

WISDOM

We exert energy doing things, offering the right touch, often forgetting the one thing that makes the most difference. Something I heard years ago speaks to me still.

On a Saturday morning, I was scheduled to speak at the Seabee Base in Gulfport, Mississippi. My eight-year-old daughter, Katie, went with me. I don't recall what other childcare arrangements I had lined up, but whatever they were didn't happen. So Katie traveled with me. I set my materials up for the seminar and seated Katie at a table close by with some markers, paper, and a book. Then I spoke about the topic which the chaplain's education director, Wanda Jensen, asked me to present, called "Growing through Grief."

I asked the workshop participants to draw pictures overemphasizing some physical attribute of themselves they believed made them a good helper to anyone going through grief. Then each person in the class showed his or her portrait and explained the magnified feature. Some had drawn huge mouths, explaining that they had comforting words to say. Others drew extra-large ears and described how they were good listeners and could hear the grieving person. Some had drawn gigantic hands and said they brought things like food or inspirational literature, or offered to babysit or mow grass.

We were wrapping up this segment of the workshop when Katie raised her hand. She had been so quiet, I had almost forgotten about her, but I said, "Yes, Katie?"

She said, "I have a picture."

I assumed that she had drawn art like we had on the refrigerator at home, but she stood up and said, "This is a picture of me, and I am keeping them company."

The room, first amused by Katie's sudden inclusion, became totally quiet. We gazed at Katie's self-portrait. She and her self-portrait were smiling.

She had been listening all along. She said it all. She would keep someone company, believe her presence would be welcome, and accept the person with whom she visited. She would be there.

Other things were said that morning. I finished what I had gone to do, and we all left. But Katie's words, more than my own, are the ones I recall.

Therapists must be the listening ear, the challenging, comforting voice, and fully present, there.

AFTERWARD

The therapeutic hour is usually forty-five minutes. The extra minutes for charting and walking one client out and another in. I don't have a particular arrangement about scheduling. Throughout the week, clients and presenting problems vary.

Imagine the waiting room of a morning scheduled only of clients who have obsessive-compulsive issues. The magazines would be neatly tidied up, the brochures put back in alphanumeric order.

Treatment is client-driven. My value system is involved and often challenged. Through the years, I have counseled both the abused and the abuser. I keep my own balance by revering humanity and following my own advice.

I believe that one tier of recovery is gratitude, which is borderless. I appreciate clients stepping up and asking for help. When I am disappointed not in a client but for a client's situation, I probe for points of encouragement.

Relationships, community involvement, work endeavors, and faith expressions can become stagnant. Noticing anew what first drew one's attention may revitalize appreciation. Recalling the details of the beginning may rekindle respect and affection. The behaviors that originally drew one to another may have become relabeled. "He is so interested in how I am doing; he calls me three times a day just to say hello" can become, "He's so nosey; he always calling me. I never have any time to myself." Rethank it.

Another tier of wellness is thinking. What one sets the mind to do often happens. Scientists can dissect and decipher the brain, but the mind is its own entity, the focal point of decision-making and action.

Establishing and continuing on the path of right thinking requires a teachable spirit. Thinking about what we have been thinking can aright malformations of thought.

In a group session for geriatric clients, a group member shared her hope about leaving the nursing home and living again, on her own, in her own home. She expressed frustration and anger, saying, "They never helped me. They only thought about themselves. They took my house."

I asked the group, "How do you manage yourself in situations you feel forced upon you?"

Another member said with an uncontrollable tremor in her voice, "You have to adjust yourself and accept that the situation is temporary."

I marveled at her words. Dwelling on pain or what lies ahead may cause one to miss the present.

Assessments attributed to human beings claiming "always" and "never" are false and may give cause for good intentions to be regarded as inadequate. No one does any one thing all the time. Reassessment of one's own thought processes may allow others the benefit of the doubt. Rethink it.

The third tier, I recognize is spiritual. I am learning to be still. Therapy is not pass or fail but a process. The "Other" in session, directing, I believe is God.

Therapy is a work in progress. When clients leave, I have the confidence that they, nor I, walk alone.

Like my client said, one needs to adjust. Life is a mixture of challenge and triumph. Revive it.

Gratitude, thinking, spirituality, and exercise are fluid tiers of adjustment. Therapy is a great enhancer of mental health.

SELECTED BIBLIOGRAPHY

Adler, Alfred. *The Practice and Theory of Individual Psychology.* Totowa, N.J.: Rowan & Allanheld, 1983.

Bandura, Albert. *Social Learning Theory.* New York: General Learning Press, 1977.

Corneau, Dr. Guy. *Absent Fathers, Lost Sons, The Search for Masculine Identity.* Shambhala, Boston and London, 1991.

Einstein, Albert. *The Principle of Relativity.* Dover Publications, Inc., 1952.

Ellis, Albert. *Feeling Better, Getting Better, Staying Better: Profound Self-Therapy for Emotional Well-Being.* Impact Publishers, Inc., 2001.

Erikson, Erik H. *Dimensions of a New Identity.* New York: W.W. Norton and Company, 1974.

Erickson, Milton H., and Jay Haley. *Changing Couples.* Triangle Press, 1985.

Frankl, Viktor E. *Man's Search for Meaning.* Beacon Press, 2006.

Freud, Sigmund. *Three Essays.* London: Hogart Press, 1905.

Fromm, Eric. *The Heart of Man.* New York: Harper & Row, 1976.

Gonzalez-Balado, Jose Luis. *Mother Teresa in My Own Words.* Gramercy Books, 1996.

Haley, Jay. *Problem-Solving Therapy.* Jossey-Bass, 1991.

Glasser, William. *Reality Therapy.* New York: Harper and Row, 1965.

Kübler-Ross, Elisabeth. *On Children and Death.* New York: Macmillan Company, 1938.

Madanes, Cloe. *Strategic Family Therapy.* Jossey-Bass, 1991.

May, G. Herbert, and Bruce M. Metzger, eds. *The New Oxford Annotated Bible with the Apocrypha.* New York: Oxford University Press, 1977.

May, Rollo. *Love and Will.* New York: W.W. Norton & Company, Inc., 1969.

_____. *Man's Search for Himself.* New York: Dell, 1953.

_____.*Power and Innocence: A Search for the Sources of Violence.* New York: Dell, 1972.

Michenbaum, D., and D. C. Turk. *Facilitating Treatment Adherence: A Practitioner's Guidebook.* New York: Plenum Press, 1987.

Minuchin, Salvador, Fishman Charles Herman. *Family Therapy Techniques.* Harvard University Press, 1981.

Shazer, de Steve, *Clues: Investing Solutions in Brief Therapy.* New York: W.W. Norton & Company, 1988.

Rogers, Carl R. *On Becoming a Person: A Therapist's View of Psychotherapy.* Boston: Houghton Mifflin Company, 1961.

Skinner, B. F. *Science and Human Behavior.* New York: The Free Press, 1953.

Sullivan, Harry Stack. *The Interpersonal Theory of Psychiatry.* Edited by Helen Swick Perry and Mary Ladd Gawel. With a foreword by Mabel Blake Cohen. New York: W.W. Norton and Company, 1953.

Tournier, Paul. *The Healing Persons.* New York: Harper and Row, 1965.

WEBSITES

www.cdc.gov/ncipc/wisqars

www.davidspeedmissions.com

www.drmaryspeed.com

www.EKBrownArt.com

www.eriphotography.com

www.northshorederm.com

www.perfectshotsphoto.com

www.sophisticatedwomanmagazine.com

www.southernbridle.com

www.twitter.com/drmaryspeed

ABOUT THE AUTHOR

I was born in a town of a few thousand people, one of the five hundred babies Nurse Doucet, the midwife, birthed and one of forty-two graduates in my high school class.

During frigid winters, my friends and I would gather inside one of our warm, cozy houses or The Blue Star Restaurant and talk. From our province of Newfoundland, "The Rock," we scattered, some fishing, some teaching, and others, like me, trying to help others figure it all out.

Mixed Nuts is an enthusiastic presentation of what I have learned.

Made in the USA
Middletown, DE
19 February 2016